Solving Your Problems Together

Family Therapy for the Whole Family

Jane Annunziata, PsyD
Phyllis Jacobson-Kram, LCSW

Illustrated by Elizabeth Wolf

American Psychological Association
Washington, DC

Published by
American Psychological Association
750 First Street, NE
Washington, DC 20002

Copies may be ordered from
APA Order Department
P.O. Box 2710
Hyattsville, MD 20784

In the United Kingdom and Europe,
copies may be ordered from
American Psychological Association
3 Henrietta Street
Covent Garden
London WC2E 8LU
England

Illustrated by Elizabeth Wolf
Designed and Typeset by
Grafik Communications, Ltd.
Printed by Palace Press International
Technical Editing and Production by
Peggy Schlegel and Susan Bedford

Library of Congress Cataloging-in-Publication Data
Annunziata, Jane.
Solving your problems together: family therapy for the whole family /
Jane Annunziata & Phyllis Jacobson-Kram; Elizabeth Wolf, illustrator.
    p.   cm.
ISBN 1-55798-268-6
1. Family psychotherapy — Popular works. I. Jacobson-Kram, Phyllis.
II. Title.
RC488.5.A56   1994   94-29708
616.89'156 — dc20   CIP

British Library Cataloguing-in-Publication Data
A CIP record is available from the British Library

Printed in Hong Kong
First Edition

Note to the Family

This book is designed to answer questions about family therapy. It explains what to expect during treatment and how such therapy can be helpful.

All families have difficulty getting along at one time or another. Ideally, family members can help each other resolve problems and handle stress. Sometimes, though, families get stuck in their problems and need help. Getting help as a family is an opportunity to look at relationships in new ways and learn to work together more effectively.

Family therapy is based on the belief that problems often result from what is taking place in relationships. Family problems are not just one person's responsibility. Family therapists believe that disruptive behaviors by individuals within families are a form of communication that needs to be understood before change is possible.

When considering what kind of help to pursue, several questions arise. Many people are not familiar with the idea of family therapy and are often reluctant to involve the entire family.

Here are some common questions and concerns:

- This is "his" or "her" problem. Why does the rest of the family have to be involved in therapy?
- Family matters are private. We should solve them ourselves, not with an "outsider."
- Does entering therapy mean that we are bad parents or that we have "failed"?
- Are the therapist and family members going to gang up on me?

In this book, we will address these questions and help you consider whether family therapy is for you.

Note to Mental Health and
Health Professionals

This book aims to familiarize people with family therapy — how it can
be useful and what can be expected from treatment. In it, we address
the typical questions that may arise when a referral is made for family
therapy. Many people know about individual therapy, but therapy
within a family context may seem like a new idea.

There are many different theoretical approaches to family therapy.
This book can be useful regardless of the theoretical orientation of the
therapist. There is no single "right" theory. What is most important
is to find the right therapist for the family.

This book can be suggested to families who are considering family
therapy or who have received a recommendation for family treatment.
It can be placed in waiting rooms where people have time to read about
different approaches to mental health problems. It is also a resource
for school, court, and medical personnel who make therapy referrals.

With love and thanks to
Gary and my parents.

Jane Annunziata

With love to David,
Halcy, and my parents.

Phyllis Jacobson-Kram

Why Family Therapy?

Family therapy is a way that families can obtain help for many different kinds of problems. It can be highly effective when people in a family have difficulty getting along with each other; when a child or teenager demonstrates behavior problems; when a family member is depressed or anxious; when parents argue too much; or when people hit, touch, or talk to each other in ways that cause anger or hurt.

What Kinds of Families
Can Therapy Help?

Family therapy can help all kinds of families—
ones with young or older children, teenagers, or
one or two parents. It can help traditional and
nontraditional families, stepfamilies, extended families,
and adults with their own parents.

Why Involve
the Whole Family?

Sometimes the need for family treatment seems obvious, such as when everyone in the family is hurting or when the whole family seems to be involved in the problems. More typically, though, one person's symptoms or behaviors are identified as "the problem." When this is the case, families are often puzzled by the recommendation for family treatment.

Family therapy is based on the belief that one person's behaviors must be understood in the context of the family. What appears to be an individual's problem can be a sign that an entire family is in distress.

Finding a
Family Therapist

How do you find a therapist who works with families? A variety of mental health professionals do this type of work.

The name of a family therapist can be obtained from a school guidance counselor, a physician, or your local mental health association. Someone you know who has been in family therapy might also recommend a therapist.

Sometimes families worry about whether they can afford to pay for treatment. If a family does not have health insurance that covers psychotherapy and they cannot afford to pay for private therapy, excellent and affordable therapy can be found at many community mental health centers and family service agencies.

Be a "good consumer." Obtain several referral names and feel free to ask questions.

Choosing a
Family Therapist

Choosing a therapist is a two-part process. Once you have the names of several family therapists, it is important to interview them by phone. Here are some important initial questions to ask:

- Do you have specific training in family therapy?
- How much experience do you have working with families?
- How long are your sessions?
- How much do you charge?

You may want to check with your insurance company to see if therapy with the individual you have chosen is covered under your policy.

The second part of the process of choosing a family therapist occurs when your family arrives in the therapist's office. Here are some questions to think about during the first meeting:

- Are each family member's ideas about the problem listened to and understood?
- Does the therapist understand what you are going through as a family?
- Does the therapist communicate clearly and in a way that makes sense to the family?
- Most important, does each family member feel comfortable with the therapist?

Concerns About
the First Session

Family members are often unsure of what to expect during their first therapy session. One of the most common concerns is when a family member refuses to attend the first meeting. Don't worry! Family therapists know how to help you encourage participation. Often this is the first problem to be addressed in treatment.

Family members also wonder whether what they say in therapy will be shared outside of the family. Family therapists, like other mental health professionals, do not share information except in unusual circumstances, such as when physical harm is a risk. If the therapist doesn't discuss this issue, ask about policies on confidentiality.

Sometimes family members worry that they will be embarrassed in their sessions. They might be concerned about arguing in front of a stranger. A family member might worry about feeling left out or blamed or fear that a family secret might be revealed. These are understandable concerns. However, your therapist is trained to deal with the stress and discomfort in these situations.

The First Session:
What to Expect

sually the therapist begins the first session by asking family members to talk about what has brought them into treatment. Each member's opinions about the family's problems are regarded as important. Each family member will be asked for his or her point of view.

Family members usually begin therapy with an idea about what is wrong with the family and what the "real problem" is. It is common for one family member to be seen as "the cause" of the problem. When things go wrong, family members often think there is a single source of blame.

New Ways to
View Family Problems

When people are blaming each other and feeling as though they have failed, it is difficult for them to see workable solutions. During the first family therapy session, therapists will try to help the family begin to find constructive ways to view their problems.

For example, parents may report that a child is disobedient or fighting too much with a sibling. They often think that the child is the only one who needs to change. In the session, the therapist might observe that when other members of the family appear tired, lack energy, and seem rather hopeless, a pattern emerges — the "problem child" acts up and only then do the other family members become alive and involved with one another.

The therapist may point out this pattern and show how the child's misbehavior may help energize the family. In this example, the therapist helps the family recognize that what seems like one person's problem is really a family

problem. Sometimes the "problem child" is really trying to help the family by distracting its members from painful matters. By just trying to "fix" the "problem child," the family may not be helping the underlying problem at all. And, as long as the underlying problem remains, it is unlikely that the "problem child" will change.

How the Therapist
Gets to Know the Family

The therapist will pay attention to what it is like to be a member of your family. For example, the therapist might notice who does most of the talking, which people in the family tend to interact the most with each other, and whether certain family members receive attention or are ignored. The therapist will try to learn how it feels to be a member of your family and what the family's "personality" is like. For example, some families are very loud and expressive, and others are quiet and restrained.

It is important for the therapist to learn about other aspects of the family's personality in the initial session. This might include cultural and religious backgrounds as well as special interests and leisure activities. A therapist needs to understand the values and beliefs that guide a family.

FAMILY
RULES

1.

2.

3.

4.

5.

Family Roles
and Rules

uring the initial session, the therapist begins to learn about the roles and rules that operate in a family.

Rules may be simple things such as who cooks the meals or who is in charge of making major decisions. Rules can include having children clean up after they play or having teenagers obey curfews. These rules are often stated, but some rules are unspoken. For example, children might sense when their parents are in "bad moods" and know that the "rule" is not to bother them, even if the children really need their help.

Roles may be less obvious, though, such as when someone is the "family comedian," the go-between, or the comforter when a family member is sad, tense, or angry.

Roles and rules can be useful to organize families, or they can lead families to feel dissatisfied or constrained. During therapy, families learn which rules and roles are uncomfortable or no longer working. They also learn to develop new rules and roles that lead to more satisfying interactions.

Family Strengths

During the first meeting, a therapist may ask what is "right" with the family. There is a good reason for this!

When families have been feeling unsuccessful at solving their problems, they often overlook the fact that there are things that are going well and things that they do well. The therapist might ask each person to think about what they like about being in the family. The therapist can help families recognize their strengths and build on them.

For example, a child who is a successful soccer player demonstrates the ability to work on a team, persevere, and cope with competition. A parent who is a good teacher demonstrates organizational skills, patience, and creativity. The therapist helps the family members apply their skills to working on their relationships and solving their problems.

What Happens
After the Initial Session?

The first meeting lays the groundwork for the later therapy sessions. When people begin family therapy, they often wonder how long it will last. This varies a great deal, depending on the type of problems, how long they have persisted, and the effect they have on the family's ability to function.

When therapy starts, the whole family generally meets with the therapist once a week. As the treatment progresses, people may be seen in different combinations. Parents might be seen without their children, siblings might be seen together, or one child might be seen with a parent alone.

Sessions can begin in a variety of ways. The therapist may ask a general question, such as how the week has been, or make an observation about how the family appears that day. Any member of the family can also raise a topic. Hearing how the week has gone gives family members a chance to learn about each others' opinions about events that took place. It reminds them of the value of listening to each other's perceptions. It also shows the therapist how the family members are feeling and communicating with each other.

What Family Members
May Learn in a Session

Based on what the family discusses and what the therapist observes, here's what often occurs:

- Family members develop an understanding of their patterns of behavior with respect to one another. This includes learning how thoughts and feelings are expressed or avoided and realizing who is generally spoken to and who is left out of family conversations. It is important for family members to understand why these patterns exist, which patterns are helpful, and which prevent them from understanding and enjoying each other.

- Family members learn about their strengths and resources and become better able to develop new strategies to resolve differences.

- Family members learn to communicate more effectively. The therapist can help them learn to listen to each other carefully, develop an understanding of each other's point of view, and find new and direct ways to share their ideas and feelings.

A unique aspect of family therapy is the chance it provides families to practice new and more rewarding ways of interacting and resolving problems in a safe place. During the sessions, family members will be asked to try out different ways of expressing themselves and different styles of responding to particular situations.

What if You
Feel Like Quitting?

Most family members, at some point in their therapy, feel like stopping before they're through. They may become discouraged about their progress, feel blamed for more than their share of the problems, or become angry at something the therapist or a family member said. This can be an opportunity to learn that there are other ways of dealing with these feelings than walking away. Therapy is like any other learning process. There are ups and downs, including times when you don't feel you are getting much out of the therapy.

Instead of dropping out, we encourage you to attend the next session and say what's on your mind. A good therapist will welcome hearing about this. No matter what your final decision, you will feel good about facing the problem rather than running away from it.

Is It Time to End Therapy?

Treatment is successful when

- the original problems or symptoms that led to treatment have mostly gone away or have greatly improved,
- family members have confidence in their ability to use their own resources to solve their problems,
- the family feels it has learned new strategies to handle present problems and future problems that may arise,
- family members feel more comfortable in relation to one another,
- the family no longer needs the therapist's help to express ideas and feelings to one another, and
- the therapist and family both agree that it is time to stop.

How Do You Know
When You Need Another Visit to
the Family Therapist?

Sometimes the entire family, the parents, or an individual wants to return to therapy. Because families go through different life stages that present new challenges, a return to therapy is not unusual. You may need more help from a therapist if

- your efforts to resolve a situation are not working,
- the problem is getting worse rather than better as you try to resolve it,
- the problem has become chronic and disruptive to family life,
- the problem is affecting the family's sense of well-being, or
- you have questions about whether you or your family need to reenter treatment.

Don't hesitate to contact your therapist by phone so he or she can help you decide whether an appointment is needed.

Conclusion

Therapy for the family can seem like hard work, but the results are far-reaching. In the course of solving problems in therapy, family members will

- feel more successful as a group and better about themselves as individuals;
- communicate more effectively within the family and with others;
- be able to stand up for themselves when they need to;
- learn to manage stress and anger constructively;
- experience less depression, anxiety, and physical symptoms; and
- get along better and feel more comfortable in close relationships.

It is in our families that we learn how to listen and how to express ourselves so that others will understand our feelings and ideas. When the whole family strives to improve in this way, each member becomes more capable of deeper and richer relationships within the family and with others.

About the Authors

Jane Annunziata has a PsyD in clinical psychology from Rutgers University. She has taught at the University of Bergen (Norway), Mary Washington College, and George Mason University. For five years she was a member of the Children's Intensive Treatment Team at the Woodburn Center for Community Mental Health in Annandale, Virginia. Dr. Annunziata is in private practice in northern Virginia (McLean), where she specializes in work with children and their families.

Phyllis Jacobson-Kram earned her MSW from Syracuse University. Her professional experience includes nine years as a family therapist at Fairfax House, a residential treatment center for teenage boys, and as a senior supervisor at the Family Therapy Center in Washington, DC. Ms. Jacobson-Kram is accredited as an Approved Supervisor of the American Association of Marriage and Family Therapy and is a certified clinical member of the National Association of Social Workers. She maintains a private practice in McLean, Virginia.